Ranma ½™

VOL. 26 **Action Edition**

STORY & ART BY
RUMIKO TAKAHASHI

RANMA 1/2

VOL. 26
Action Edition

Story and Art by
RUMIKO TAKAHASHI

English Adaptation/Gerard Jones
Translation/Kaori Inoue
Touch-Up Art & Lettering/Wayne Truman
Cover and Interior Design & Graphics/Yuki Ameda
Supervising Editor/Michelle Pangilinan
Editor/Avery Gotoh

Managing Editor/Annette Roman
Editor in Chief/Alvin Lu
Production Manager/Noboru Watanabe
Sr. Dir. of Licensing & Acquisitions/Rika Inouye
VP of Marketing/Liza Coppola
Sr. VP of Editorial/Hyoe Narita
Publisher/Seiji Horibuchi

RANMA 1/2 is rated "T+" for Older Teens. It may contain violence, language, alcohol or tobacco use, or suggestive situations.

Printed in Canada.

Published by VIZ, LLC
P.O. Box 77010
San Francisco, CA 94107

Action Edition
10 9 8 7 6 5 4 3 2
First Printing, April 2004
Second Printing, April 2004

store.viz.com

STORY THUS FAR

The Tendos are an average, run-of-the-mill Japanese family—on the surface, that is. Soun Tendo is the owner and proprietor of the Tendo Dojo, where "Anything-Goes Martial Arts" is practiced. Like the name says, anything goes, and usually does.

When Soun's old friend Genma Saotome comes to visit, Soun's three lovely young daughters—Akane, Nabiki, and Kasumi—are told that it's time for one of them to become the fiancée of Genma's teenaged son, as per an agreement made between the two fathers years ago. Youngest daughter Akane—who says she hates boys—is quickly nominated for bridal duty by her sisters.

Unfortunately, Ranma and his father have suffered a strange accident. While training in China, both plunged into one of many "cursed" springs at the legendary martial arts training ground of Jusenkyo. These springs transform the unlucky dunkee into whoever—or whatever—drowned there hundreds of years ago.

From now on, a splash of cold water turns Ranma's father into a giant panda, and Ranma becomes a beautiful, busty young woman. Hot water reverses the effect...but only until next time. As it turns out, Ranma and Genma aren't the only ones to take the Jusenkyo plunge—and it isn't long before they meet several other members of the Jusenkyo "cursed."

Although their parents are still determined to see Ranma and Akane marry and carry on the training hall, Ranma seems to have a strange talent for accumulating surplus fiancées...and Akane has a few stubbornly determined suitors of her own. Will the two ever work out their differences, get rid of all these "extra" people, or will they just call the whole thing off? What's a half-boy, half-girl (not to mention all-girl, *angry* girl) to do...?

CAST OF CHARACTERS

RANMA SAOTOME
Martial artist with far too many fiancées, and an ego that won't let him take defeat. Changes into a girl when splashed with cold water.

RYOGA HIBIKI
Melancholy martial artist with no sense of direction, a hopeless crush on Akane, and a stubborn grudge against Ranma. Changes into a small, black pig Akane's named "P-chan."

GENMA SAOTOME
Ranma's lazy father, who left his wife and home years ago with his young son (Ranma) to train in the martial arts. Changes into a panda.

SHAMPOO
Chinese-Amazon warrior who's gone from wanting to kill Ranma to wanting to marry him. Changes into a cute kitty-cat when splashed.

NODOKA SAOTOME
Ranma's mother and Genma's wife...only, she doesn't know Ranma is sometimes a girl, and her husband sometimes a panda. Has previously vowed to assist in the *sep-puku* (ritual suicide) of them both should Ranma turn out anything less than "manly."

COLOGNE
Shampoo's great-grand-mother, a martial artist, and match-maker.

HAPPOSAI
Martial arts master who trained both Genma and Soun. Also a world-class pervert.

AKANE TENDO
Martial artist, tomboy, and Ranma's reluctant fiancée. Has no clue how much Ryoga likes her, or what relation he might have to her pet black pig, P-chan.

RANKO
Ranma's "girl-type" alter-ego, especially with his (unsus-pecting) mother.

SOUN TENDO
Head of the Tendo household and owner of the Tendo Dojo.

RYU KUMON
Angry young martial artist who's ingratiated himself into Ranma's mother's household—the better to avenge himself against Ranma.

CONTENTS

Part 1

MOTHER, I AM RANMA

ITOKYU
THE BIG SALE
BEARS·OHMY!
INTERIORS
GIRLS SALE
I HATE THIS...
NOT WITHOUT HAVING TO...
I CAN'T EVEN VISIT MY OWN MOTHER...
SIIIGH
WELL, RANKO?
SHOOF

GIRLS
OOO, DO YOU REALLY THINK SO, MA'AM?
IT'S SO... GIRLISH!
RANKO, DEAR! IT'S ADORABLE!
GO AHEAD AND LAUGH.
LUCKY YOU... RANKO.
WE'LL TAKE THIS.
SIIIIGH
MRS. SAOTOME... YOU REALLY MISS RANMA, DON'T YOU.
HOW LONG WILL IT BE BEFORE RANMA COMES HOME...?
OH, DEAR...
DEPT STORE
ITOKYU
THE BIG
I CAN'T WAIT TO SEE HIM, ALL GROWN UP AND MANLY!
HE IS MY ONE AND ONLY SON.
SIIIGH

CREPES
C'MON, RANMA—
WHY DON'T YOU JUST TELL YOUR MOM WHO YOU ARE?
PST PST PST
SHE FINDS OUT I'M HALF-GIRL, IT'S SEPPUKU-TIME.
WHO CARES ABOUT A BELLY OR TWO?
I ONLY HAVE THE ONE.
EEEEK
AAAAH
A BEAR!!
A BEAR'S ESCAPED!!
HM?
BEAR?
RAAAR
BEARS•OH MY!
A VERY SPECIAL EXHIBIT

FREEZE!!

NN?

HUH !?

BWAK
BWAK
KLATT
BEARS:
VERY SPECI
KLATT

SHWUMMP
DMP
WHAT THE HECK WAS THAT MOVE... ?!
WHAT... ?

YOU OKAY, LADY?
WH-WHY, YES, THANK YOU...
AND WHAT'S YOUR NAME...?
HM...?
WHAT A MAN...!
LATER.
JUST PASSING BY, NO NEED FOR A NAME.
THAT YOUNG MAN MUST HAVE...
TM TM

OH MY !
TH- THIS IS...
Ranma Saotome

HUF HUF

.....
WHAT COULD'VE HAPPENED? SHE LOOKED SO SHOCKED...

CONSTRUCTI
HUH ?
UM, EXCUSE ME...

THANK YOU...
MY SECRET SCROLL! YOU'VE NO IDEA HOW...
B-BMP B-BMP
HEY !
IS THIS...
Ranma Saotome
Stupid Pops
OH, THE BEAR LADY.
TP TP TP

"THOUSAND-MOUNTAIN PATH."
SAOTOME SCHOOL, ANYTHING-GOES...

OH, THAT.
UM... THAT ATTACK YOU USED...
SNEAK
?

...ANY-THING... GOES ??
SAOTOME... SCHOOL...

RANMA SAOTOME.

TH... THEN COULD IT BE... ?
PLEASE... YOUR NAME...

RA...

WHAT !?

RANMA!! OH, YOU **HAVE** GROWN UP MANLY !!

GOOSH

EH ?

WE WERE PARTED WHEN YOU WERE SO SMALL... YOU DON'T REMEMBER!
BUT I AM YOUR MOTHER !
MY... ?

MOTHER!!

GOOSH

RANMA!!

WH...
WHAT THE HECK IS GOING ON!?
BRRR BRRR

GRRR
WUF WUF

THE POOR HOUSE WE USED TO LIVE IN LONG AGO HAS BEEN DEMOLISHED...
YOU DON'T REMEMBER, DO YOU.
I WAS JUST A BABY...

......

WHO IS HE, ANYWAY !?
THAT CHUMP! USING MY NAME AND SNEAKING INTO MY MOM'S PLACE...

I heard it all.
POP
SO YOU'RE HERE.
HUH ?

YEAH... UH...
WEREN'T YOU ON A TRAINING TRIP TOGETHER... ?
WHAT OF YOUR FATHER ?
THAT REMINDS ME...
OH, RANMA.
腹

WHAT !?
...DIED.
DAD... KINDA...

切腹

CARE FOR SOME RICE CRACKERS ?
SURE.
切腹

Could she be any less upset?!
POPS, SHH! QUIET...
KLOMP KLOP

KREEE..
VOOP

UP THERE !!
CHOOP

SOMETHING THE MATTER, RANMA?
NOPE...

OWOO WOW WOW

REE
REE
REE...

HA.

LUCK IS ON MY SIDE.
I'D GIVEN UP HOPE THAT ANY MEMBER OF THE SAOTOME CLAN WOULD ANNOUNCE THEMSELF TO ME.

AND NOW THAT I'VE INFILTRATED THE SAOTOME HOUSE...
I'LL FIND THE SECRET SCROLL WITH THE **MISSING MATE** TO THE "1000 MOUNTAIN PATH."
Ranma Saotome
Stupid Pops

HEY YOU.

WHO ARE YOU ?

THOUSAND-MOUNTAIN
VS. THOUSAND-SEA

HYOOO
I DUNNO WHO YOU ARE...
BUT DO YOU THINK YOU CAN CHALLENGE **RANMA SAOTOME** AND ACTUALLY WALK AWAY UNHURT!?
"RANMA SAOTOME," HUH...?
HA!

OOO
WOOF
WOOF
USING MY NAME AND FOOLING MY MOM-!!
MOTHER!!
RANMA!!
YOU'RE GONNA PAY!!
VSH
GLINT

FREEZE!!
SKWIK
"FIERCE TIGER GATE-OPEN BLAST" !!
BAP
BIP
NKH !

TO EVADE MY "YAMA-SEN KEN" BY A HAIR'S WIDTH...
YOU'RE PRETTY GOOD !

"1000 MOUNTAIN" MY **FOOT** !
ZK
DISTRACTING ME WITH ALL THAT STUPID SHOUTING...

YOU'RE NOT WORTHY TO FIGHT UNDER THE NAME **SAOTOME** !!
WAK WAK WAK
HOH.
HOH.

!!

FWAH

OH... ?

WIDE OPEN.

MOM...

OH NO !

...?

"DEADLY SNAKE-PIT PROBING PALM" !!

THOG

SH... SHOOT...

BOM
WAGH !!

BOING
PING

HE GOT AWAY.
TSK.

HWOOOO

A SMOKE-SCREEN !?
BAM

BUT I TOOK CARE OF HIM.
BURGLAR, MAYBE...

WAS THERE SOMEONE HERE...?
WHAT'S THE MATTER?

MOM.
RANMA...
CHIRING

YOU'RE NOT WORTHY TO FIGHT UNDER THE NAME **SAOTOME** !!
IS THAT GUY RELATED TO THE SAOTOMES...?

OWOOO
WOF
WOF

YOU LET YOUR GUARD DOWN, MORON.

YOU ALMOST HAD YOUR HEART TORN OUT.

POPS...
THIS "YAMA-SEN KEN," YOU HEARD OF IT?

HEARD OF IT?
I **INVENTED** IT.
WHAT !?

I DON'T KNOW HOW HE GOT HIS HANDS ON THE "1000 MOUNTAIN" SECRET SCROLL, BUT...
A FIGHTING STYLE SO VIOLENT, IT HAD TO BE SEALED AWAY!

SO WHY IS HE PRETENDING TO BE ME AND STAYING AT MOM'S PLACE?

HIS GOAL IS MOST LIKELY...
...THE MATE TO THE YAMA-SEN KEN—THE **UMI-SENKEN** SCROLL!
"1000 **SEAS**"...?

AND WHERE **IS** THIS SCROLL?
WELL, IF IT HASN'T BEEN THROWN AWAY BY NOW...

THE SAOTOME SCHOOL'S SECRETS !!
YOUR MOTHER SHOULD HAVE IT.
I'M NOT LETTING THAT JERK GET 'EM !!
MRS. SAOTO-O-OME !
TA TA TA TA
OH, RANKO! HELLO, DEAR.
UMI-SEN KEN... ?
COULD I HAVE A WIDDLE PEEK AT THE UMI-SEN KEN SCROLL?
SINCE RANMA IS HOME, WE'RE HAVING A FEAST!
NEVER MIND THAT, MRS. SAOTOME.
WOULD YOU LIKE TO HAVE DINNER WITH US ?

AND WHAT IS THAT ?
HUH... ?
D-TOMP BOMP
BAM

CURSES !
I CAN'T FIND IT !
VAP VAP VAP
UMI-SEN KEN AND YAMA-SEN KEN ARE TWO SIDES OF ONE COIN.
YAMA-SEN KEN SECRET SCROLL
IT IS SAID THAT ONLY AFTER MASTERING BOTH WILL ONE ATTAIN A PERFECT ATTACK.

HRAAWR!
TM TM
HOO HOO HOO HOO HOO
NO MATTER WHERE THE "1000 SEAS" SCROLL IS HIDDEN... MY STEALTH WILL UNCOVER IT!!

RANMA! DINNER-TIME.
PAT PAT
WAAAAAGH !!

OH MY, SUCH A MESS! NO TIME TO CLEAN UP NOW.
AFTER DINNER, THOUGH, PLEASE.
B-BMP B-BMP B-BMP
Y-YES.... MOM.
HARDLY SUBTLE, IS HE.

AHAHAHA!
SUCH A BOY!

HOW CAN HE GET AWAY WITH THIS ?
I'M STILL SAFE !
PHEW

RANKO DEAR, AFTER DINNER, LET'S YOU AND ME TAKE A NICE, HOT BATH TOGETHER.
EEK !

WHAT ?
BYE !
I JUST REMEMBERED SOMETHING I'VE GOT TO DO.
TM TM TM

RANMA, COULD YOU RUN AFTER LITTLE RANKO FOR ME?
OH, THAT'S RIGHT...

I BOUGHT IT BECAUSE IT WILL LOOK SO CUTE ON HER.
PLEASE GIVE HER THIS RIBBON.
GEEZ.

HUH ?
ZHIPP

THAT GIRL'S GOT SOME FAST LEGS.
GONE ALREADY...

TUP TUP
WHAT'S WITH HER...?

SHE'S NOT YOUR AVERAGE GIRL !!
THOSE LEAPS...

SO WHERE THE HECK IS IT!?
I THINK MOM REALLY DOESN'T KNOW ABOUT THE YAMA-SEN KEN SCROLL....

PEEK

YOU'RE BACK, EH?
TP

BLORB BLORB
FOOEY.

WHY DO I, THE **REAL** SON, HAVE TO RUN AWAY FROM HIS MOM!?

RRGH! ARGH

WE MADE A PROMISE NOT TO TALK ABOUT THAT.

KLONG

I NEVER MADE ANY PROMISE!

WHAT!?

THE GUY FROM YESTERDAY...

HE'S THE REAL RANMA SAOTOME!?
WHAT'S GOING ON HERE!?

Part 3

RANMA VS. RANMA

YOU'RE STILL LETTING THAT **FAKE** RUN AROUND!?
BLAH BLAH
THIS WOULD ALL BE OVER IF YOU'D JUST BE HONEST WITH YOUR MOM, RIGHT!?
OH SHUT UP!

DOOOM
POK
POK
KLATT
THE FAKE RANMA!
GASP
WHA-!?

HEY, MR. REAL.
WHAT...
HUH? WHA? WHO?

I DON'T KNOW WHAT YOUR STORY IS...
BUT I GATHER YOU CAN'T TELL YOUR MOM WHO YOU REALLY ARE, RIGHT?
!

MY REAL NAME IS **RYŪ KUMON.**
THE MAN WHO **WAS** TO BE THE HEIR TO THE KUMON DOJO.
THAT'S ALL YOU NEED TO KNOW ABOUT ME.
KUMON...?

YOU WANT ME TO TELL YOUR MOM THAT YOU'RE HER REAL SON?
WH-WHY, YOU...!

I'M GONNA **CRUSH** YOU!!
VSH

HA!
WHRL

DUM
DON'T RUN AWAY, YOU !!
YAAAH!
EEEEK!

I COULDN'T FINISH YOU LAST TIME...
SO LET'S SETTLE THIS NOW.

HWOOO~
RRRMMBL

AFTER I WIN, YOU'RE LEAVIN' MY MOM'S HOUSE!
YOU GOT THAT !?

HEH...
YOU'RE PRETTY CONFIDENT, HUH?

JAB
YOUR "YAMA-SEN KEN"...
I KNOW ABOUT ITS SECRETS !!

DO YOU.

THE INITIAL, STARTLING YELL IS THE KEY.
FREEZE!!
AFTER STOPPING THE OPPONENT IN HIS TRACKS, THE REST IS RELATIVELY EASY.

A PURE, BRUTE-FORCE ATTACK!

IT AGGRESSIVELY TEARS THRU THE OPPONENT'S GUARD...

I SEE... WELL, IF YOU'RE SO CONFIDENT...
RRRMMBL
HEY! IT'S MOM!!
WHA...
PWIK
DMM
AGH!!
SWOP

BOOT

WHY, YOU !!

ZF

PAP

"FLIGHT OF THE TIGHT-BIND GOLDEN THREADS" !!
FSH
GH !?
WOOP LOOP

IF YOU **WANNA** SEE A BRUTE-FORCE ATTACK...
I'LL **SHOW** YOU !
GWEEP

"FANGED FINGERS OF STEEL WELCOME-GATE"!!

DOOK

AH...

UMI-SEN KEN AND YAMA-SEN KEN ARE TWO SIDES OF THE SAME COIN. HOWEVER...
UMI-SEN KEN IS **FAR** MORE ADVANCED.
TEACH ME UMI-SEN KEN, THEN!
I'M GONNA SMASH HIM!
I CANNOT TEACH YOU.

JUST LIKE YAMA-SEN KEN, UMI-SEN KEN IS A SINISTER SKILL THAT OUGHT HAVE BEEN DESTROYED.

AS SOON AS THE SECRET SCROLLS ARE FOUND, THEY WILL BE BURNED!!

MAYBE YOU DON'T KNOW, MAYBE YOU'RE PRETENDING.
DON'T CARE, EITHER WAY.

I'LL PLAY THE PART OF THE SON UNTIL I FIND THE "1000 SEAS" SCROLL.
RGH...
SHF

DON'T GET TOO CLOSE TO YOUR MOM'S HOUSE.
OR I'LL EXPOSE YOU.

SSHHH—...
HUFF HUFF
GASP
DANG IT...
D...
ZOOP---
RANKO...?
WHAT'S WRONG?!
RANKO DEAR, IT IS YOU!!
MOM...

POOR RANKO, YOU'RE **HURT**!
AND COVERED IN MUD.
COME BACK TO MY HOUSE AND...
MRS. SAOTOME...

JUST FOR A LITTLE WHILE...
...I WON'T BE ABLE TO SEE YOU.

WHAT...?

OH...
TA TA TA

SHH

DON'T WORRY.
I'LL COME VISIT SOON ENOUGH!
RANKO...?
PLISH PLOSH
THE 1000 SEAS PATH IS MORE ADVANCED...
...AND TROUNCES 1000 MOUNTAIN!!

天道道場
TENDO DOJO
KU...
KUMON DOJO, YOU SAY!?

IM SURE THAT WAS IT.
MY REAL NAME IS RYŪ KUMON.
THE MAN WHO WAS TO BE THE HEIR TO THE KUMON DOJO.

WH...
WHAT CRUEL TWIST OF FATE IS THIS...

DOM DOM DOM

KLATTAH!
POPS !!

RANMA! THOSE WOUNDS...
ARE THOSE FROM THAT RYŪ GUY...!?
SHP

RANMA...DO YOU HAVE THE CONFIDENCE IT TAKES TO MASTER THE PATH OF 1000 SEAS??

SO... **NOW** YOU'RE READY TO TEACH ME, EH !?

Part 4
INTENSIVE
TRAINING!!

HWOOO—
THE "1000 SEAS" PATH OF THE SAOTOME STYLE... A TERRIBLE SKILL THAT OUGHT HAVE BEEN SEALED AWAY FROM THE BEGINNING...
I WILL TEACH THIS ONLY ONCE.
THIS IS WHAT I WILL BE PASSING ONTO YOU.
ONCE SHOULD BE PLENTY.
HE MUST REALLY BE AFRAID OF THIS GETTING OUT....
NO PEEKING
Genma Saotome
HE'S LOCKING US OUT, EVEN.... ?

IF THE "1000 MOUNTAIN," WITH ITS BROAD MOVES AND BRUTE FORCE, EMBODIES "STRENGTH"...

THEN "1000 SEAS" IS **SUBTLETY.**

SMALLER, QUIETER...

...AND DEMANDING A SKILL MUCH MORE ADVANCED.

NOW... COME AT ME FROM WHEREVER YOU WANT.

PFF

!

EH !?
SAOTOME'S "KI"...
HIS **PRESENCE**... JUST VANISHED !?
NO PEEKING Genma Saotome
SS—HH
THAT STANCE...
LIKE A GHOST...
HERE I COME, POPS !!
VM
!?
PFF

WH...
!?

GWOOP
SS—HH
NO PEEKING
Genma Saotome
EEP!

RANMA...
!?
IT'S OVER ALREADY
!?
SOMEONE SHOULD TEND TO RANMA...

R-RANMA!!

OH... OH, MY...

THE SECRET OF "1000 SEAS" IS...
...SMALLER... QUIETER...

IM GONNA MASTER THIS...
NO MATTER WHAT IT TAKES–IM GETTIN' MY MOM BACK!

THE CONNECTION BETWEEN ME AND THE KUMON DOJO... ?
SORRY, BUT...
REE REE KRIIIKET KRIIIKET REE REE

MY REAL NAME IS RYŪ KUMON.
THE MAN WHO WAS TO BE THE HEIR TO THE KUMON DOJO.
WHY WAS RYŪ NO LONGER ABLE TO TAKE OVER THE DOJO?

FOO...
ONE SIMPLE REASON.

BECAUSE MY "1000 MOUNTAIN"...
...ERASED THE ENTIRE KUMON DOJO FROM THE FACE OF THE EARTH.
WH-WHAT !?
IT ANNIHILATED A WHOLE SCHOOL-?
BUT I NEVER GUESSED...

THAT ANYONE COULD CLAIM TO BE ITS HEIR.
RYŪ...
FIND THE SECRET SCROLL... OF "1000 SEAS"...

UMI-SEN KEN... YAMA-SEN KEN...
ONCE YOU'VE MASTERED THEM, THE REBIRTH OF OUR DOJO...WILL NO LONGER...BE A DREAM.
DO YOU... UNDER... STAND... ?
FOMP
DADDY !
DADDY !!
I'VE TURNED THIS HOUSE INSIDE OUT WITH NO LUCK.
...WELL, IF THAT'S THE CASE...
RANMA !
DINNER'S READY !
切腹
TKK
IM SORRY THIS HAS TO BE DONE...
BUT IM GONNA HAVE TO TIE HER UP AND MAKE HER TELL !

WHAT'S WRONG, RANMA?
SMILE

LOOM

THANK YOU, RANMA.
OH, THAT FEELS SO NICE.
SIIIGH
RUB RUB
RUB RUB
IM TOO SENTI-MENTAL.
RGH...

AKANE, YOUR TURN TO TAKE A BATH.
'KAY.

WEIRD. I THOUGHT HE WAS OUT COLD.
HEY, RANMA...

!

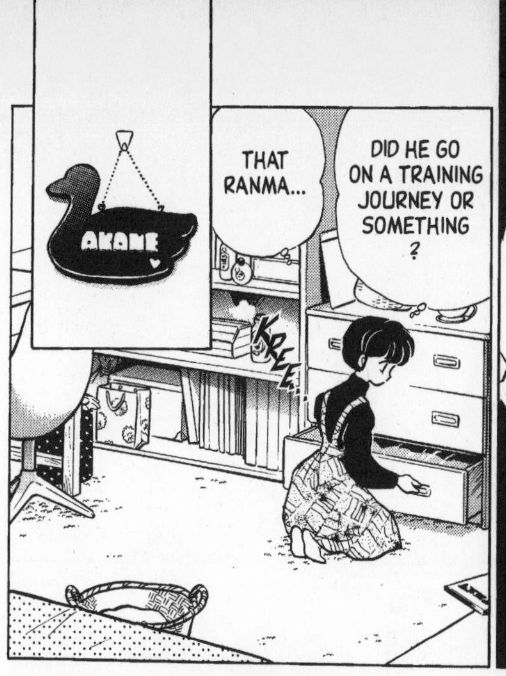
DID HE GO ON A TRAINING JOURNEY OR SOMETHING ?
THAT RANMA...
KREE
AKANE

VEGETABLES IN MY UNDERWEAR DRAWER... !?

CREEEP

EVEN IN MY DESK...
GRRK

STUFF HERE, TOO !?
KLAK
CREAM
HAM
BUTT

SO YOU'RE BEHIND THIS !!
K-SHAWM!
DARN. SHE SAW ME.

AT LAST, A MINUTE TO READ THE PAPER.
FLAP

CREEEP

WHERE'S RANMA ?
BEATS ME.

WOMP

DID SOME-ONE...
JUST STEAL OUR FOUNDATION... ?

HE HAS MASTERED THE WAY OF UMI-SEN KEN !!
AFTER JUST ONE PUNCH...

EVEN FOR MY SON, THIS IS AMAZING !!
GASP
RANMA !

IS "1000 SEAS" TRAINING !?
Y-YOU MEAN ALL THIS...

SEAL THIS AWAY, AND SEAL IT SOON.
"TERRIBLE SKILL" IS RIGHT !
WHAT A PAIN.

AKANE.
PING

CAN THIS KIND OF THING POSSIBLY DEFEAT RYŪ?
COME ON...

HWOOO—

WSH

RANMA!? WHERE-!?

I'M IN THE MIDDLE OF TRAINING.

BUT I HAVE A FAVOR TO ASK YOU...

ALL RIGHT.

ASK ME. BUT FIRST...

SHOW ME YOUR FACE.

DO YOUR BEST.
I'LL BE ROOTING FOR YOU.
OH...
AKANE...
SIIGH

PICK SOMEWHERE **ELSE** FOR YOUR STUPID TRAINING!
OOG...

NOW, WHAT'S THIS FAVOR?
I'LL DO WHAT I CAN.
O... KAAAY....

HELLO, MRS. SAOTOME.
!
OH, AKANE !
SHE'S A FRIEND OF THE REAL RANMA.
IF I REMEMBER...
MY... FIANCÉE !?
IT'S YOUR FIANCÉE, AKANE.
LOOK, RANMA !
......
......

Part 5

A LETTER FROM MOTHER

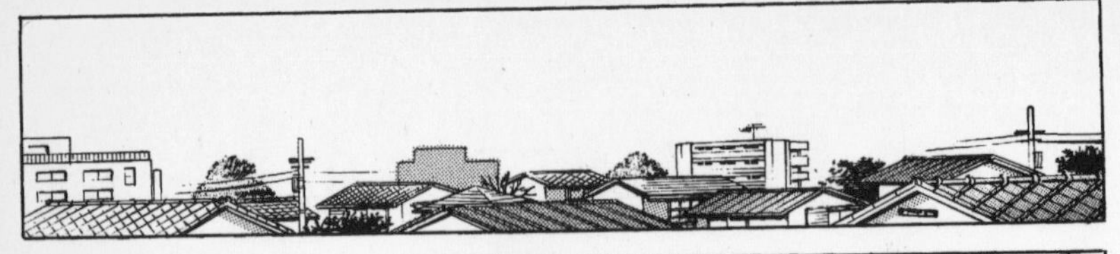

.....
SURELY YOU MUST BE HAPPY TO SEE AKANE.
OH, COME NOW...

SHE MUST BE HERE TO EXPOSE ME...

...MAYBE NOT.
OR...

LONG TIME NO SEE.

EHEH

YOU SURE GOT CUTE SINCE I SAW YOU LAST !
YO, AKANE.
GOOSH

I'LL JUST RUN ALONG AND BUY SOME GROCERIES !
SINCE I'M NOT NEEDED HERE...
ZIP

HURRY HOME !
JAB

SO...

THIS...
WHAT ARE YOU HERE FOR ?

A LETTER OF CHALLENGE FROM THE REAL RANMA.
Challenge

TOMORROW MORNING AT 5 A.M.... ?
FWIP

I WILL BATTLE YOU WITH THE UMI-SEN KEN.

THINK OF ME AS A LIVING "1000 SEAS" SCROLL.

IF I LOSE, THE SECRET TECHNIQUE WILL BE YOURS. BUT IF YOU LOSE...

YOU WILL BURY THE "1000 MOUNTAIN" PATH ALONG WITH IT.

HA, THIS IS PERFECT!

A BATTLE BETTING EACH OTHER'S FIGHTING STYLES!

AND ONE MORE THING.
AHEM
JERK

"PLAYING WITH MY MOTHER'S HEART JUST FOR SOME DUMB SCROLL...
"IS A CRIME I CAN NEVER FORGIVE !

"I'LL MAKE YOU PAY FOR THAT DURING THIS MATCH, DO YOU HEAR ?!!"

OR SO HE TOLD ME TO TELL YOU.

HAVING A NICE TALK ?

...SHE DIDN'T HEAR...
B-BMP B-BMP B-BMP
IS... THAT SO... ?
HUF HUF HUF
SHOPPING WENT VERY QUICKLY....

OH.
AKANE DEAR, ARE YOU GOING HOME ALREADY?
I-I'M ALL DONE HERE...
ONE THING.
SLIPPA SLIPPA
HERE...
THIS LETTER.
COULD YOU GIVE IT TO LITTLE RANKO?
SLIPPA SLIPPA
THE LAST TIME WE MET, SHE DIDN'T LOOK HER LIVELY SELF.
I'M WORRIED.
I KEEP THINKING ABOUT HER...

THANK YOU, MRS. SAOTOME.
WHAT...?
SKWEEZ

RAN...
...KO WILL BE VERY PLEASED, I'M SURE.

I'M HOME! WHERE'S RANMA?
STILL IN THE MIDST OF HIS TRAINING, I SUPPOSE... THERE'S NO SIGN OF HIM.
天道道場
TENDO DOJO

AKANE

WHERE COULD HE BE?
...KLIK

ZIP ZIP

I TOLD YOU NOT TO DO YOUR WHACKED-OUT TRAINING IN OTHER PEOPLE'S ROOMS!
OOG

...FROM MOM?

SHE SEEMED WORRIED ABOUT YOU.

SHK

HOW ARE YOU, RANKO?

I'm sad that you haven't been by so I can see your girlish face.

TH-THIS IS THE SECRET "UMI-SEN KEN" SCROLL!!

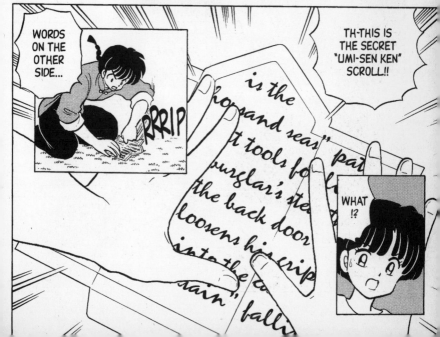

WORDS ON THE OTHER SIDE...

RRRIP

is the

the back door

WHAT !?

THAT LETTER WAS MEANT FOR RANKO, NOT...!!
WHAT'S GOING ON!?

COULD IT BE THAT MOM...
...KNOWS WHO I REALLY AM?

SSHFF...

HWOOO~~

KRAK!
THEN I MUST FURTHER HONE MY "1000 MOUNTAIN' PATH !!
IF THE "1000 SEAS" PATH IS TO BE MINE WITH THIS MATCH...
SAOTOME SCHOOL OF ANYTHING-GOES MARTIAL ARTS–YAMA-SEN KEN ULTIMATE ATTACK...

"DEMON-GOD MULTIPLE STRIKE" !!
KOOM
T-TAK
BZZT
BZZT
ZUDDD

RYŪ...FIND THE SECRET SCROLL... OF "1000 SEAS"... DO YOU... UNDER... STAND...?
FOMP
DADDY! DADDY !!
DAD...
WE'RE ALMOST THERE...

I'VE TRAVELED ALONE SINCE I WAS A SMALL CHILD.
IN ORDER TO FIND THE UMI-SEN KEN...

THE WARMTH OF ANOTHER'S PITY...
I GREW UP NOT KNOWING...

MUCH LESS THE FACE OF MY MOTHER...
OR THE HOT TEARS THAT TOUCH ONE'S HEART.

TMP
NOT SINCE I WAS BORN...

I WAS WORRIED, YOU WERE SO LATE.

WELCOME BACK.

DINNER'S READY.

LET'S HURRY HOME.

YES...

COME OUT, YOU STUPID POPS!!
POPS!

SO HE RAN OFF, THE COWARD!!
CRUMPLE

HE JUST SLUNK OFF ON A TRIP.
IF YOU WANT SAOTOME...

天道道場
TENDO DOJO

IF WHAT THIS PART SAYS IS REALLY TRUE...
THIS PIECE OF THE SCROLL MOM SLIPPED ME...
RRR
THAT OLD MAN IS DONE!!

EARLY NEXT DAY

MWIP

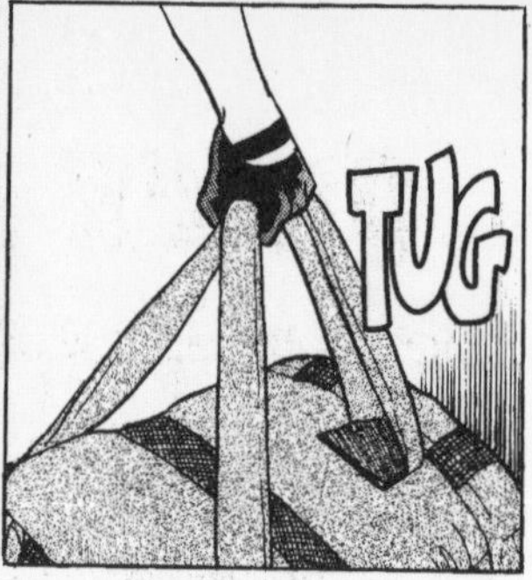
TUG

THERE'S NO REASON FOR ME TO STAY HERE ANYMORE.
SEE YA, LADY.

JUST A MOMENT.
!
TP

Part 6

QUICK AS LIGHTING-THE THOUSAND SEAS!

TIK
TOK
TIK
TOK
WHAT'S WITH THE SWORD...?
WHAT IS THIS?
DOES SHE KNOW I'M AN IMPOSTOR...?
WELL...

MY SON...
SINCE THE "1000 SEAS" WILL BE MINE VERY SOON.
NO MATTER...
UH...
AS A WARRIOR, YOU MUST HAVE SOME HIGHER GOAL.

!
IS IT IN ORDER TO ATTAIN THAT GOAL?
THIS FIGHT...

FOR I AM A WARRIOR'S WIFE.
WHEN IT IS TIME FOR A MAN TO GO INTO BATTLE, I CAN SENSE IT.

WALK THE PATH THAT YOU BELIEVE IS TRUE.
AS LONG AS YOU FEEL PRIDE IN IT...
GNG
BOW
CHEE CHEE...
ZSH...

I'M ON MY WAY TO BEAT UP YOUR SON.

I'LL DO JUST THAT, LADY.
HUH.
AS LONG AS YOU FEEL PRIDE IN IT...
WALK THE PATH THAT YOU BELIEVE IS TRUE.
KRAK

Z-ZZSSHH

ZZSSH...
TODAY WILL BE "1000 MOUNTAIN"'S LAST, YOU FAKE.

I'VE COME FOR THE "1000 SEAS."
Don't Hurt The Buddha
NOW WE BEGIN THE BATTLE BETWEEN...
...THE UMI-SEN KEN AND YAMA-SEN KEN OF THE SAOTOME SCHOOL. BUT FIRST...
RYŪ KUMON!
POING

NO.

BECAUSE I WON'T LOSE.

IF YOU LOSE, YOU APOLOGIZE TO MY MOM!

YOU TELL HER YOU **TRICKED** HER!

Hss..

HMPH...
FINE WITH ME.

AND ANOTHER THING!

YOU GET ON YOUR HANDS AND KNEES AND APOLOGIZE TO **ME**, TOO!
.....

AND THEN...
YOU RUN AROUND TOWN...
WEARING A SIGN THAT SAYS, "I'M A FAKE!"
FAKE RANMA ROUTE
OGAWA
THERE'S THAT FAKE RANMA!
I'M A FAKE
TSK TSK!
WHAT A LOSER!
YEAH! WHY DON'T YOU JUST...
GAH!
NOT THAT I'D EVER CALL YOU PETTY, BUT...
RANMA, I THINK THAT'S A BIT MUCH...

OOM
SHUT UP !!
"FIERCE TIGER GATE-OPEN BLAST" !
THOK
ZIP

KRAKK
BOK BOK
THOOOOOOOOOOM
TP

THAT MASSIVE PINE... SPLIT LIKE A PAIR OF CHOP-STICKS!
THE YAMA-SEN KEN... FISTS OF STRENGTH!!

EVEN IF HE DID DODGE THAT ONE...
CAN RANMA'S UMI-SEN KEN REALLY PROTECT HIM FROM SUCH BRUTE FORCE!?

HWOOO—
SHK
Don't Hurt The Buddha
PLAYING IT COOL, HUH?
YOU MISSED THAT FIRST STRIKE ON PURPOSE, DIDN'T YOU?
WHAT!?
HEH.
IF I TOOK YOU OUT IMMEDIATELY...
I WOULDN'T GET TO SEE THE "1000 SEAS" IN ACTION.

THIS IS MY...

WHOA !
WHEN DID... ?

FSS
THE SUBTLETY OF UMI-SEN KEN.

YOU CAN'T STOP...

PFF...

WHAT YOU CAN'T SEE.

THAT STANCE...

RANMA'S **KI** JUST VANISHED !

IS THIS A JOKE!?
VSH
SSS

VYOOOFF

BAPBAPBAP
GH... !?

DOM

TP

TH-THIS IS...

JUST LIKE WHEN RANMA WENT THROUGH THE TRAINING...

SAOTOME SCHOOL-UMI-SEN KEN-

"STRIKE OF THE SPITTING WHITE SNAKE"!

COULD YOU SEE IT?

KH...!

TO LEARN THESE BLOWS ONE AT A TIME WITH MY BODY...
GLINT
...WOULD BE TOO MUCH... SO....

"FLIGHT OF THE TIGHT-BIND GOLDEN THREADS" !!
VWAH

WHY DON'T I JUST BEAT YOU TO A PULP AND MAKE YOU CONFESS ?

GWEEK

WHY, YOU... !!

Part 7

HOUSE OF THE SEA, HOUSE OF THE MOUNTAIN

TUG
FSH
"FANGED FINGERS OF STEEL WELCOME-GATE"!!
HE'S GOING TO SEIZE HIS HEART—!
NO!
AAGH!

"SLASHING ARMORED FANGS OF FURY" !!

FSH

"STANCE OF THE COLLAPSING BRACE" !!

PWAH

SHP

"STRIKE OF THE SPITTING WHITE SNAKE" !!

BAPBAPBAP

KH...

OH !

I'M SEEING IT !
WHAT'S BEHIND "1000 SEAS" AND "1000 MOUNTAIN" !!
WHAT... !?

IT'S A **HOUSE** !

BOTH FIGHTING STYLES EQUATE THE PHYSICAL BODY WITH A HOUSE!

ROOF

FRONT DOOR

A HOUSE... !?

GATES

BACK DOOR

SUPPORT BEAM

FOUNDATION (UNDER FLOOR)

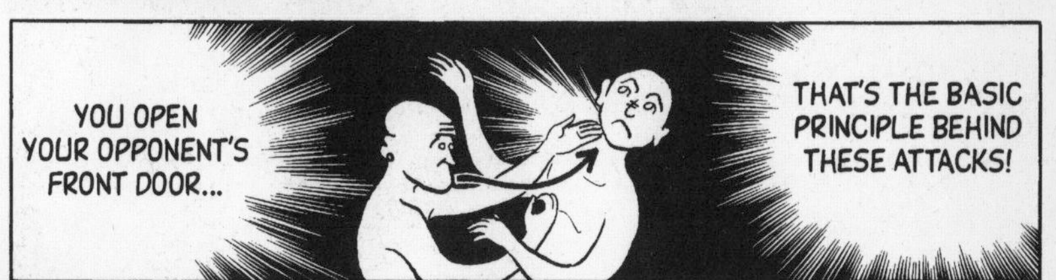

YOU OPEN YOUR OPPONENT'S FRONT DOOR...
THAT'S THE BASIC PRINCIPLE BEHIND THESE ATTACKS!

THUS, RYŪ'S "1000 MOUNTAIN"...

"FIERCE TIGER GATE-OPEN BLAST" !!

...IS LIKE GAINING ENTRANCE BY CRASHING HEADFIRST THROUGH THE FRONT GATES.

GWARPA

BAM

BY CONTRAST, RANMA'S "1000 SEAS"...

...ERASING ONE'S OWN PRESENCE IN ORDER TO ATTACK FROM AN OPPONENT'S BLIND SPOT...

...IS LIKE SLIPPING THROUGH THE BACK DOOR AND DESTROYING THE ENEMY FROM WITHIN!!

THOSE COUNTLESS, STRANGE TRAINING EXERCISES IN THE HOUSE...

THAT REMOVAL OF THE FOUNDATION...

"STANCE OF THE COLLAPSING BRACE"!

THE LIGHTNING-QUICK OPENING AND CLOSING OF DRAWERS...

"STRIKE OF THE SPITTING WHITE SNAKE"!

THEY WERE ALL PART OF SLIPPING THROUGH THE DEFENSES!

I CAN'T BELIEVE THAT LAZY SAOTOME ACTUALLY CREATED A COMBAT STYLE AS INCREDIBLE AS THIS...
I THOUGHT ALL HE COULD DO WAS LIE AROUND...
CAN IT BE HE'S GOT REAL POWER AFTER ALL...?

BLOOM!
HEH HEH HEH. ALL THIS PRAISE IS MAKING ME BLUSH!
YOU GETTING IT NOW...?
UMI-SEN KEN?
WHERE HAVE YOU BEEN HIDING!?
MMMG
SAOTOME! YOU ARE SUCH A...
UGH...

WHAAAT !?
WOBBLE...
I GET IT...
I GET ITS FATAL WEAKNESS, AT LEAST... !

I SEE...

THEN, RYŪ KUMON, YOU'RE A DANGEROUS MAN!
IF HE'S REALLY CAUGHT ONTO IT...

UH...
IS THERE REALLY A WEAKNESS TO UMI-SEN KEN?
MR. SAOTOME...

SNEER

WHY DON'T YOU TEACH ME THEN, THIS SUPPOSED WEAKNESS?
SSSS...

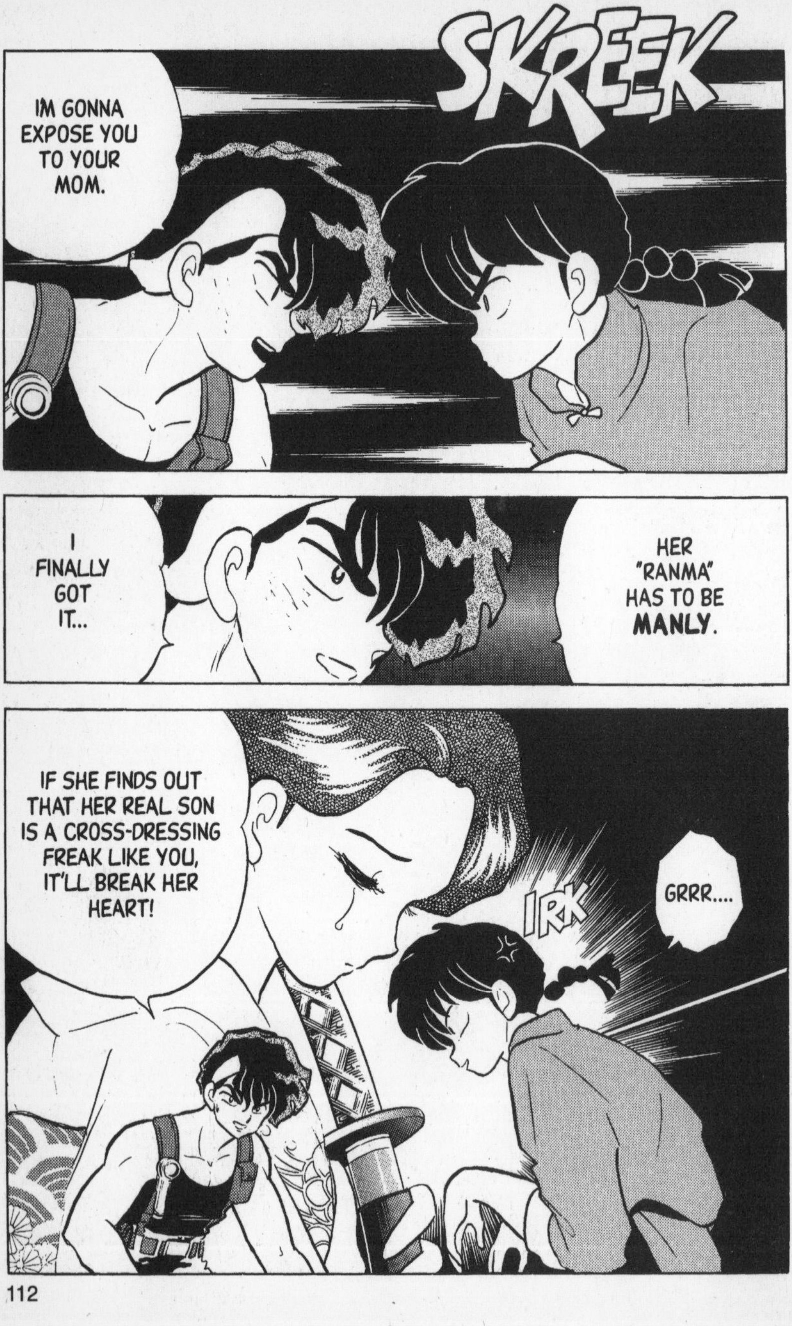

GRRR....

IRK

IF SHE FINDS OUT THAT HER REAL SON IS A CROSS-DRESSING FREAK LIKE YOU, IT'LL BREAK HER HEART!

DO YOU THINK I'D ACTUALLY FALL FOR SOMETHING AS...
HWOOOSH

...DUMB AS THAT !!
VSH

RANMA, NO !

BUT WITH ANGER, RANMA HAS FALLEN INTO RYŪ'S TRAP...
THE SECRET IS TO ERASE ONE'S "KI," ONE'S PRESENCE, AND MOVE INTO THE OPPONENT'S BLIND SPOT.

IF THAT GOES ON...
PLUS, HE'S EXUDING A FIGHTING "KI" OF RAGE!
VSH

ZIP

DONG

NKH!

I SEE IT!

KRRRK

"CRUSHING EMBRACE OF THE KILLER GRIP" !!

OH NO! HE'S CAUGHT !
RANMA !!

KH-*
MAYBE I SHOULD JUST KEEP GOING AND BREAK THAT SPINE OF YOURS!
MOOSH

D...
DAMN
IT...
KATAK
KATAK
GLUE
PEP
切腹
SHP
TAP

MY BEST TEA CUP...
KTONK
BAD LUCK...
SOME-THING'S WRONG...
IF YOU DON'T GIVE UP—YOU'RE GONNA **DIE**!
KH...
GRNNNH
CAW CAW
FLAP FLAP FLAP

FSH

I'VE GOT NO CHOICE !!

OHH !!

TH-THAT'S... !!

Part 8
THOUSAND-MOUNTAIN TRAGEDY

FSH

"CLOTH OF FALLING STARS" !!

RANMA!! YOU'RE USING **THAT** !?

SOMETHING'S COMING OUT OF HIS HANDS...

SWSH
!

TUG
GAH!!

HE'LL **STRANGLE** HIM!
WHAT DESPERATE MEASURES!!

KH...
JKK

HIS GRIP LOOSENED!! NOW...

"CARP BODY FLIP"!!
FOOP

IT'S AN OFFENSE AND DEFENSE IN ONE!
GOOD! NOW KEEP THE MOMENTUM GOING AND TAKE HIM DOWN!!
ONE ATTACK FLOWS INTO ANOTHER!!
"MOUN-TAIN FALLING INTO SEA"!!
GNG
GRAH!!

FSH
KWRL

"TIGHT-BIND GOLDEN THREADS"!!
PONG

RRRIIP
OH YEAH!?

IF THIS CONTINUES, THEY'LL BOTH BE...
IF...
GYOO

BOING
BAH!
DAD !?

SSSNIP
PING

DZZZ

SHK
WHAT ARE YOU DOING !?
HAK HAK

HIT THIS MAN !!
EH ?
?
GWIP

HE IS THE ONE WHO CREATED UMI-SEN KEN AND YAMA-SEN KEN.
HE'S THE TRUE OBJECT OF YOUR REVENGE.
HE DIDN'T HAVE TO KNOW THAT!
REVENGE ?

THIS IS GENMA SAOTOME. THE MAN WHO USED THE "1000 MOUNTAIN" PATH...
...TO DESTROY THE KUMON DOJO THAT YOU WERE TO TAKE OVER.
PAT PAT
WHAT ARE YOU TALKING ABOUT?

I DON'T KNOW THAT OLD OCTOPUS-HEAD.
AND BESIDES, THE ONE WHO DESTROYED THE DOJO IN THE FIRST PLACE...

...WAS MY OWN FATHER.

SIGH

!?

WH...

WHAT DO YOU MEAN!?

IT'S TRUE.

I GAVE ONLY THE YAMA-SEN KEN SECRET SCROLL TO HIS FATHER.

WHAT!?

VOOP

WE WERE POOR.

OUR DOJO WAS LITERALLY LEANING.

60° ANGLE

THEN ONE DAY...
RYŪ!
I'VE OBTAINED A GREAT SCROLL!
KREE KREE
TIP-TOE TIP-TOE

FATHER SAID IT WAS BEQUEATHED TO HIM BY A KINDLY, TRAVELING MARTIAL ARTIST...
IF WE MASTER THIS "1000 MOUNTAIN PATH," OUR DOJO MAY BE REBORN!!
REALLY, DADDY?

I SEE...
A TECHNIQUE THAT EQUATES THE HUMAN BODY WITH A **HOUSE**...
WELL. LET THE TRAINING BEGIN!
Ranma Saotome Stupid Pops

"FIERCE TIGER GATE-OPEN BLAST" !!
WOK
WAM
"DEADLY SNAKE-PIT PROBING PALM" !!
DOK
"CRUSHING EMBRACE OF THE KILLER GRIP" !!
KRAK
SUPPORT BEAM
AND SO...

THE DOJO THAT HAD BEEN BARELY STANDING... COLLAPSED.

KLONK KLONK

WUMP

DADDY !
DADDY !!
FOMP
RYŪ...
FIND THE SECRET SCROLL... OF UMI-SEN KEN... DO YOU... UNDER... STAND...?

STOP CALLING ME THAT.
JAB
SO TELL ME THIS, OCTOPUS-HEAD...

THAT'S TRUE, ISN'T IT!?
IF UMI-SEN KEN AND YAMA-SEN KEN ARE USED TOGETHER, OUR DOJO CAN BE RESTORED, RIGHT?

BUT...
IT'S TRUE...

HUH...

!

HOOSH...

HA--- ------ ------

VOOOOM

HIS KI... SUDDENLY INCREASING...
VOOM
RUN FOR IT!!
OH NO!

SAOTOME SCHOOL, "1000 MOUNTAIN" ULTIMATE ATTACK...
KRAK

"DEMON-GOD MULTIPLE STRIKE" !!
DOOOOM
RANMA, YOU IDIOT!! RUN!!
PEEK

BASH
!
BASH
BASH
OH...

BDMMMM

HE SLICED THROUGH THE STATUE WITH HIS **FISTS** !!
KTAK TAK
WH- WHAT !?

FEH...
SIZZLE
UGH...

NOW... IF YOU VALUE YOUR LIFE...
TELL ME THE SECRETS OF THE 1000 SEAS.
KRAK KRAK

YOU...
YOU'RE USING YOUR SKILLS FOR THE **WRONG** REASONS.

WHAT !?

YOU'RE USING THEM JUST TO DESTROY THINGS...
NOT TO **CREATE** ANYTHING...
WOBBLE...

UMI-SEN KEN AND YAMA-SEN KEN...
THEY'RE TOOLS FOR **LIVING**!!
LISTEN TO ME, AND LISTEN GOOD.

LIVING!?

TAKE ANOTHER SHOT WITH YOUR...
"DEMON-GOD MULTIPLE STRIKE ATTACK."
FYOO!..
NOW YOU'LL LEARN THE SECRETS WITH YOUR OWN BODY.

HUH !?

SHK SHK

MOM... WHY **NOW**... ?

SHK

MRS. SAOTOME !?

Part 9
THE INVISIBLE STRIKE

SHE'S COMING !!
SHK
SHK
SHK
IF SHE SEES ME, IT COULD BE A CATASTROPHE !!
UH-OH.
WHAT BRINGS HER HERE... ?
STRANGE...

ZOMPF

HYOO
ROO
ROO

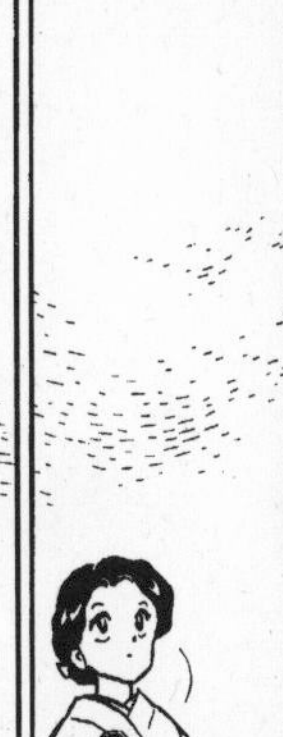

THIS SENSE OF FORE-BODING ?
WHAT COULD BE CAUSING...
SHK
SHK

We need to talk.
GRAB
OH, MR. PANDA... WHAT'S WRONG ?

ACK !

Hurry up and end this.
PAP

FLING
VROOM

DOOM
YAGH !
"DEMON-GOD MULTIPLE STRIKE" !!
NO !
KRIK KRAK
DZZZ

WHY YOU~~~!

ARE YOU THAT SCARED OF YOUR MOM?

YOU LET YOUR GUARD DOWN.

GWIP

I DON'T HAVE A SECOND TO LOSE !!

MOOF

"MEGA-CLOTH OF FALLING STARS"!

IT'S OVER !!
DOOM
ZIP
!?
KKKK
RANMA...
HE'S GONE ?!
SH——HH
TK

SSHH...
PWIK...
GOT YOU !!
THOK
ZIP
ZIP
OH NO, YOU DON'T.
PFF
URK
!
FSH
FOOP

ACK !
WHAT !?

WHAT'S RANMA TRYING TO ACCOMPLISH !?
I DON'T GET IT !!

HUH !?

THE RESULTING VACUUM CREATES **SHARP KNIVES OF AIR** THAT SLICE THROUGH OPPONENTS!!
VACUUM
RYŪ'S "DEMON-GOD MULTIPLE STRIKE" USES, IN ESSENCE, THE ACTION OF **FLINGING OPEN SHUTTERS** TO FORCE APART THE AIR ITSELF...

SO HOW CAN STEALING RYŪ'S CLOTHES...

FOOP
...COUNTERACT SUCH A DEADLY ATTACK !?

IT'S NOT **JUST** CLOTHES...
OH !

THE ROCKS THAT BROKE OFF THE SCULPTURE...

AH-CHOO

ARE GONE, TOO !?

ZIP

THAT IDIOT, UP TO HIS TRICKS...

ZIP

ZIP

SAOTOME SCHOOL "1000 MOUNTAIN" ULTIMATE ATTACK No. 2!!
NG

NUMBER 2 !?

"VIOLENT DANCE OF THE DEMON-GOD HORDE" !!

PA PA PA PA PA PA PA PA

WRLLL

ZSH
ZSH
HE'S STRIKING AT RANDOM !!
B-B-B

BOOOM...
MY !
TEE-TEE TEE-TEE
CLEVER MR. PANDA !
THANKS FOR SHOWING ME YOUR NEW TRICK!
CLAP CLAP
Did you enjoy it?
WELL NOW...
I MUST BE GOING.
Wh- where to?

SINCE I CAN'T SHAKE THIS FEELING OF FOREBODING, I CAME TO PRAY.
DOOOM BOOM
NO NO NO NO!
TAK TAK

SSSS SSSS

PFF—

CURSE HIM...!

SNEAKING AROUND LIKE A **RAT**!

COME OUT!!

I THOUGHT I TOLD YOU ALREADY...
YOU CAN'T **FIGHT** WHAT YOU CAN'T **SEE**.

TIME TO SEAL YOUR "1000 MOUNTAINS" AWAY!
NOW, YOUR YAMA-SEN KEN...
LOOM
WHAT !?
HERE I COME !
VMM
THE MEGA-FURO-SHIKI...
OH !

"ULTIMATE DEMON-GOD MULTIPLE STRIKE" !!
FWAH
YES !!
DOES THE FOOL THINK HE'LL SQUASH ME... !?

SAOTOME SCHOOL "1000 SEAS" ULTIMATE ATTACK...
"DEEP-SEA DEMON WRAP" !!
BAM
BAM
THE GROUND'S BEING SUCKED **UPWARD** !?

Part 10

THE TRUTH OF THE SECRET SCROLLS

ZHHHHHH
HMMMM
WHAT IS HE DOING!?
I... I THINK I SEE...
BY STUFFING THE FUROSHIKI...
SIMULTANEOUSLY LOOSENING THE GROUND AROUND HIM...
AND THEN BLOCKING THE VACUUM CREATED BY RYŪ'S ATTACK WITH HIS HUGE BUNDLE...

GET READY TO BE BURIED !!
AND IS WRAPPING EVERYTHING IN DIRT !
PULLING AIR UPWARD FROM EVERY DIRECTION, WHICH SUCKED UP THE LOOSENED EARTH...
RANMA APPLIED PRESSURE TO THE VACUUM FROM ABOVE...
VACUUM
DDDMMM

HYOOOO—
THAT'LL TEACH YOU...
KLUNK
ZHEH ZHEH
RANMA...
HE WON !!
BLAST IT !
WOK
.....
AS PROMISED, WE WILL SEAL AWAY YOUR "1000 MOUNTAIN PATH."
AGREED ?

THE UMI-SEN KEN AND THE YAMA-SEN KEN...
THEY'D NEVER HAVE DONE WHAT YOU WANTED.
RYŪ... WHAT I TOLD YOU IS TRUE.
WHAT DO YOU MEAN !?
THEY ARE TOOLS FOR LIVING, NOT FIGHTING.
TMM
HE MEANS THAT EVEN THOUGH THEY ARE BOTH TERRIFYING ATTACKS...
YOU'RE BACK...
SAOTOME...

AT LAST !

THE TIME HAS COME TO SPEAK.
HEAR THE TRUTH BEHIND THE SCROLLS !!

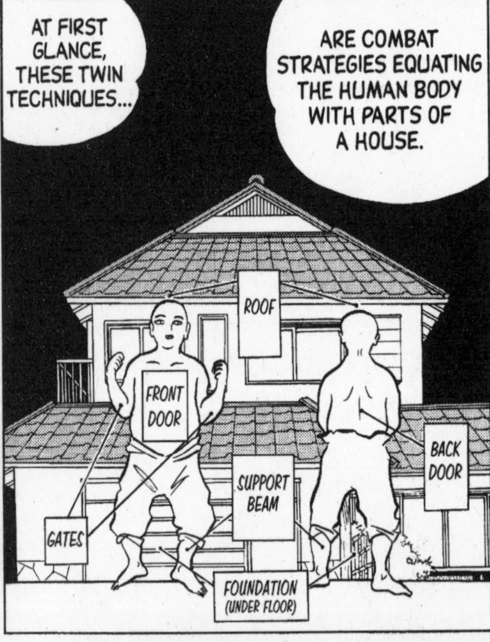
AT FIRST GLANCE, THESE TWIN TECHNIQUES...
ARE COMBAT STRATEGIES EQUATING THE HUMAN BODY WITH PARTS OF A HOUSE.
ROOF
FRONT DOOR
BACK DOOR
SUPPORT BEAM
GATES
FOUNDATION (UNDER FLOOR)

"FIRST GLANCE" !?

THE SECRET SCROLL OF UMI-SEN KEN.
THIS IS WHAT MOM GAVE ME.

FAP
To Ranko

WHSH

THE THOUSAND SEAS !?
FWAP

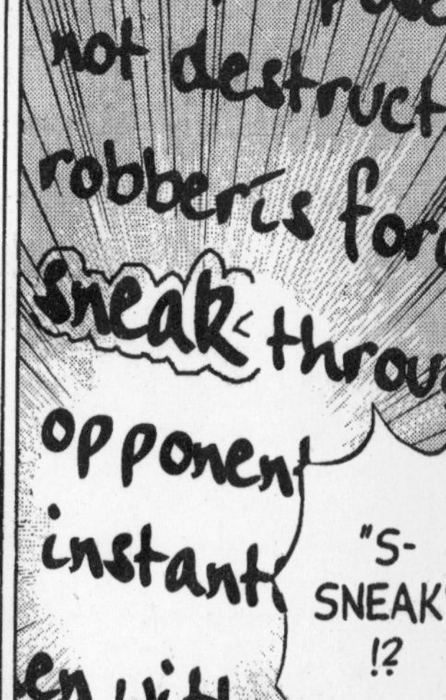
purpose
not destruct
robber is for
sneak throu
opponent
instant
en with
"S-SNEAK" !?

...FEH
BRRR BRRR
To Ranko

OH !

YES. YOU SEE...
"1000 MOUNTAIN" IS A TOOL FOR A **ROBBER** TO FORCE HIS WAY INTO A HOUSE FROM THE FRONT DOOR.
FREEZE!!
BAM
EEEEK
"1000 SEAS" IS A TOOL FOR A **BURGLAR**...
...TO SNEAK IN AND STEAL WITHOUT DETECTION.
ZIP ZIP ZIP
R-ROBBER...?
AND A BURGLAR...?
THESE ARE "TOOLS FOR **LIVING**"!?
BRR BRR

RGH.
RANMA STOLE THE VACUUM CREATED BY YOUR MULTIPLE STRIKE.
DON'T YOU SEE?

HOW DOES A BURGLAR USE THAT LAST ATTACK! ?
DON'T LIE TO ME!
OH, THE DEMONIC WRAP...

YOUR POOR FATHER...
SIGH

THEN RESTORING THE KUMON DOJO WOULD NOT HAVE BEEN JUST A...
PLOP
PLOP
PLOP
IF HE'D UNDERSTOOD THE TRUTH OF YAMA-SEN KEN HE COULD'VE STOLEN A FORTUNE!!

UMI-SEN KEN AND THEIR CREATOR...
...HAVE FINALLY BEEN SEALED AWAY.
ZUD

SHFF...
!?
NO...
WHAT I'VE STRUGGLED AGAINST ALL THIS TIME...
FLOP
MRS. SAOTOME...
M-MOM !?

LADY
!!
BA-BOOM

VSH
MOM
!!

FOR
SHAME
!
Slipped her a mickey. She was in the way.

PLEASE
!!
LADY! SNAP OUT OF IT!!!

ACK
!
"LADY"...
?

THAT STUPID~~~!
SHK SHK
SHK...
I WAS ALREADY BEGINNING TO SUSPECT...
YOU'RE NOT THE REAL RANMA.
!
OH...
WHAT !?
PEEK
WELL... PECULIAR...
YOUR REACTION TO YOUR FIANCÉE AKANE WAS...

THANK YOU.
I DID ENJOY IT.
I...
LADY...
ALMOST AS IF I'D REALLY FOUND MY RANMA.
BUT IT WAS...
I'M SORRY...
OH, MOM...
AH...!
IF YOU **REALLY** WANT TO MEET YOUR SON—!!
BUT...

THE REAL RANMA...

.....

...MAY BE CLOSER THAN YOU THINK.

IF I EVER DO MEET HIM...

I'LL BE SURE HE KNOWS HOW YOU FEEL.

SHUP

TAKE CARE.
GOOD-BYE.
GRP
SEE YA.
BETTER TELL HER THE TRUTH SOON.
SHK
SHK SHK
FAREWELL, LADY.
YEAH...

FFP
THE SECRET SCROLL...
DID MOM SEND IT BECAUSE SHE KNOWS I'M RANMA...?

OH, THAT...?

THIS ENVE-LOPE...

UM~
AHEM
OH! RANKO DEAR.

IT'S A SCROLL MY HUSBAND SENT WHILE HE WAS TRAVELING, WITH THE NOTE, "GET RID OF THIS THING."
SO YOU'RE REUSING IT!
Always so practical...
MRS. SAOTOME, YOU'RE THE VERY MODEL OF A POOR MARTIAL-ARTIST'S WIFE.
PLEP PLEP
FOLD

Part 11
RANMA'S TEARS

RANMA, YOU HAVE BORNE ALL MY HARSH TRAINING WELL.
THERE IS NO MORE THAT I CAN TEACH YOU.
PLISH PLISH
WHAT ARE YOU SO GRIM ABOUT, OLD MAN...?
OLD ONE! 'TIS TIME! COME ABOARD!
AH. MY ESCORT PARTY HAS ARRIVED.
PLISSSH
THEN HAPPOSAI IS...
WAIT...IS THIS THE RIVER STYX...?
OH!
PLISH PLISH
THIS IS GOODBYE, RANMA.

REST IN PEACE, OLD MAN! REST IN...
I UNDER-STAND! I WON'T STOP YOU!

SPLOOSH
AUGH! COLD!
GASP

YO. YOU GOT A FEVER OR SOMETHING?
UH-HUH.
"SIZ-ZLE"?
HUH?
GOOD MORRR-NING, RANMA!
SIZZLE

I FEAR I'VE COME DOWN WITH A COLD...
SNIFFLE
KOF KOF
IF YOU'RE NOT FEELING GOOD...

STAY IN YOUR **OWN** STUPID BED!
VROOM
BOING

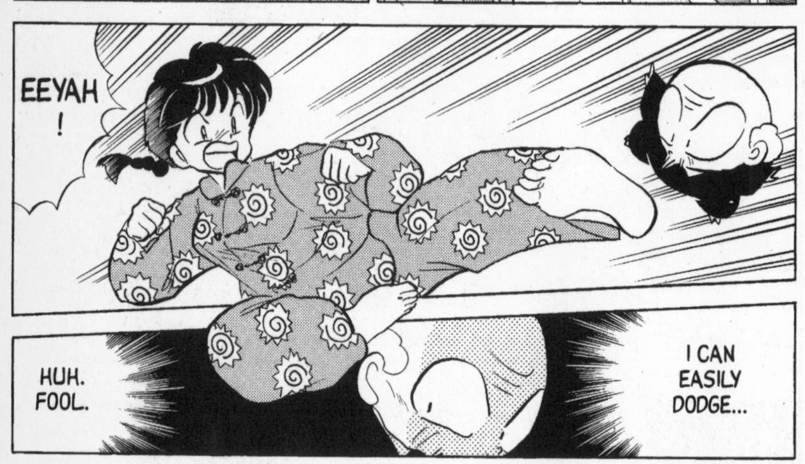
EEYAH!
HUH. FOOL.
I CAN EASILY DODGE...

HUH?
SPLAT
GAH!?

WHY, YOU-!
WRLLL

HAPPO-FIRE BURST!
FSHH
SSSS

TONG
CH-BOOM
HA! TAKE THAT, YOU OL' GOAT !
CRAWL CRAWL
.....
HUH ?
PLOD PLOD
HE'S NOT FIGHTING BACK...?
DON'T WORRY ABOUT ME...I'LL RECOVER...
HEY. WERE YOU ACTUALLY SERIOUS ABOUT BEING SICK?

CAT WHISKER. LIZARD TAIL.

DUMPLING SKIN. FALCON CLAW.

GARLIC. AND CARROT.

GRUNN GRUNN

THIS IS COLD MEDICINE?

EHE-HE-HE-HEH.

FOOL.

IT'S THE "POTION OF YOUTH."

PING

Y... YOUTH!?

NOW, IT'S COMPLETE!

GEHEHEHEH

BRACE YOURSELF, RANMA!

YOU SHALL PAY FOR WHAT YOU'VE DONE!

GLOB GLOB GLOB GLOB

BOM!

I'M **SURE** IT SAID GRIND THEM TOGETHER...
WHEEZ WHEEZ
POTIONS
SOME-THING'S NOT RIGHT.

EH?
POTIONS

I MISSED THE MOST IMPORTANT INGREDIENT!
GASP
H-HOW COULD THIS BE...?

STUPID OLD GEEZER...
A YOUTH POTION?
WHAT? I SENSE...

TEAR GAS !?
DRIP DROP

IS THIS...
HAK HAK
KOFF

BA-BA-BAM
ACK !
BWAH !

AGH !
WSH

JUST SHUT UP AND HAND OVER THE TEARS.
GEHEHEHEH
ZHEE-HEE ZHEE-HEE
WHAT'S THIS ABOUT !?
YOU GOAT !
TUP
BOING

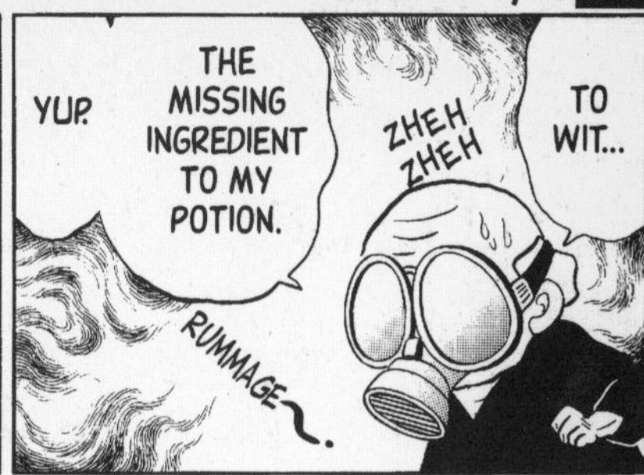
TO WIT...
ZHEH ZHEH
THE MISSING INGREDIENT TO MY POTION.
YUP.
RUMMAGE~.

TEARS !?
RUB

IN OTHER WORDS- **YOUR** TEARS, RANMA !
SHOOP
THE TEARS OF A FABLED BEAST, AT ONCE MALE AND FEMALE!
PIPETTE

KWOP

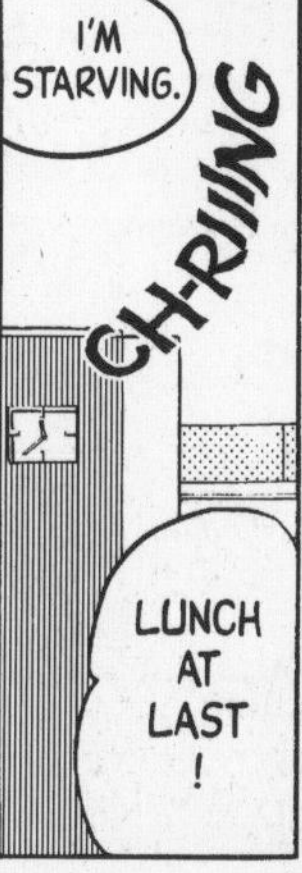
I'M STARVING.
CH-RIIING
LUNCH AT LAST !

WHO YOU CALLING A "FABLED BEAST" !?
BOOT

GAH.

YOU DIMWIT !
KRASSSH
THEEERE WE GO! RUBBY RUBBY.
GOOSH
PYOOO
ONIONS !?

YOUR ORDER, SIR !!
FAP FAP
FAP
ZOOP
I WILL NOT GIVE UP!

YOU WANT IT, IT'S YOURS.
I'M JEALOUS, RANMA.
YUM YUM
HEY, SUSHI !

DON'T... PUSH ME...
HOW DARE YOU REFUSE MY KINDNESS...?
BO~~NG
WHEEZ WHEEZ
DRIP DROP
AUGH! WA... WASABI !

YOU'RE SICK! STAY IN BED!

GOOSH

SIZZLE

YAH! H-HOT!

HMMM...

THE ICE MELTED ALREADY.

WHEEZ WHEEZ

OLD MAN.

IM SORRY.

I DIDN'T THINK YOU WERE THIS SICK.
WHEEZ WHEEZ
R... RANMA...?

IF MY TEARS WILL REALLY HELP...
THEY'RE YOURS.
AAH. RANMA'S TEARS.
MASTER. CAN YOU HEAR ME?
HE'S DELIRIOUS WITH FEVER!
YOU NEED THE TEARS OF A FABLED BEAST BOTH MALE AND FEMALE??
SOBB
THEN TAKE OUR TEARS! ALL YOU WANT!
AS MUCH AS YOU WANT !!
BLOP BLOP
SKRIIIK

KA-BASSH
YOU JUST TOOK **YEARS** OFF MY LIFE!

BOOSH
GAAH !?

THE TEARS ARE MINE!
PLOSH PLOSH
WHAT IS THIS !?
GEH HEH HEH
PSSHHH...
I PUSHED THE PRESSURE-POINT FOR THE TEAR GLANDS!

STOP, YOU GEEZER!
DM DM DM
WRA-HAHAHA! ETERNAL YOUTH IS IN MY HANDS!

OOP.
TRIP
OOSH

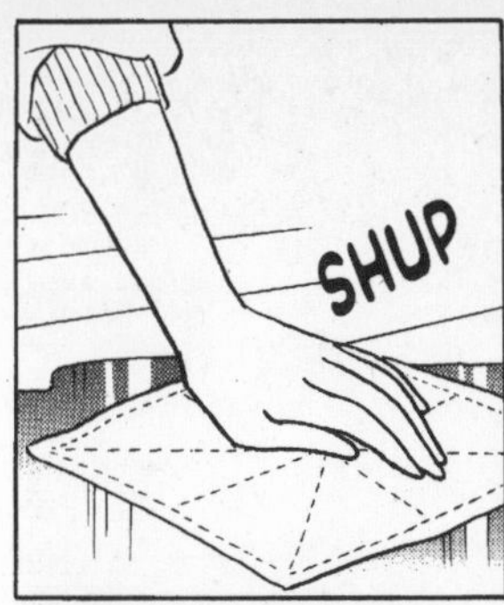
SHUP

DON'T WORRY, YOU POOR OLD DEAR. I WAS CLEANING UP ANYWAY.
WIPE WIPE

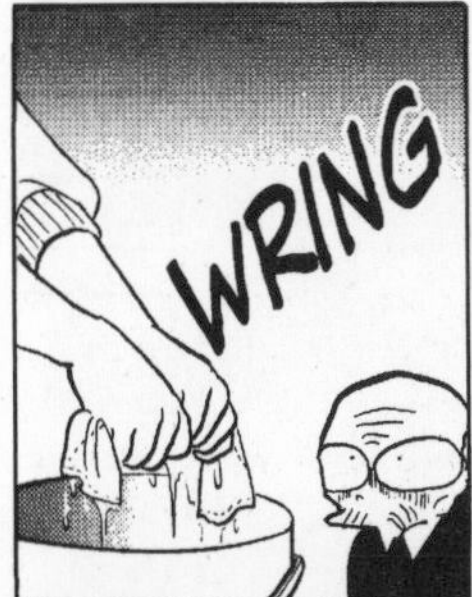
WRING

AND ME WITH MY TEARS DRIED UP.

KLONK

OLD MAN.
HEY, OLD MAN. HANG ON.

PLOOSH
HERE. IT'S THE YOUTH POTION.
IS THAT... THE TEARS...?
WAIT...

WE ALL PITCHED IN TO WIPE IT UP.
UNFORTUNATELY, THE CLOTHS HAD SOY SAUCE ON THEM.
I'D NEVER FORGIVE MYSELF IF YOU DIED ON ME AFTER ALL THIS.
I'M GOING ON A TRIP!
WOBBLE
WHY, YOU...

SO NOW YOU'RE **TOO GOOD** TO DRINK MY TEARS ?!

BLOOOSH

GLUB GLUB GLUB

PING

OOOH!

IT REALLY WORKED!!

I'M NOT SURE THIS IS WHAT HE HAD IN MIND.
MAYBE IT'S A DOSAGE PROBLEM.
BABA.
BOOBY.
HE'LL BE WITH US A WHILE.
MAN! THAT IS ONE **CREEPY** BABY!

—RANMA 1/2 Volume 28 • The End—

COMPLETE OUR SURVEY AND LET US KNOW WHAT YOU THINK!

☐ Please do NOT send me information about VIZ products, news and events, special offers, or other information.

☐ Please do NOT send me information from VIZ's trusted business partners.

Name: ______________________________

Address: ______________________________

City: ____________ **State:** ______ **Zip:** ______

E-mail: ______________________________

☐ **Male** ☐ **Female** **Date of Birth** (mm/dd/yyyy): ___/___/______ (Under 13? Parental consent required)

What race/ethnicity do you consider yourself? (please check one)

☐ Asian/Pacific Islander ☐ Black/African American ☐ Hispanic/Latino

☐ Native American/Alaskan Native ☐ White/Caucasian ☐ Other: ______

What VIZ product did you purchase? (check all that apply and indicate title purchased)

☐ DVD/VHS ______________________________

☐ Graphic Novel ______________________________

☐ Magazines ______________________________

☐ Merchandise ______________________________

Reason for purchase: (check all that apply)

☐ Special offer ☐ Favorite title ☐ Gift

☐ Recommendation ☐ Other ______________

Where did you make your purchase? (please check one)

☐ Comic store ☐ Bookstore ☐ Mass/Grocery Store

☐ Newsstand ☐ Video/Video Game Store ☐ Other: ______

☐ Online (site: ______________________________)

What other VIZ properties have you purchased/own? ______________________________

____

How many anime and/or manga titles have you purchased in the last year? How many were VIZ titles? **(please check one from each column)**

ANIME	MANGA	VIZ
☐ None	☐ None	☐ None
☐ 1-4	☐ 1-4	☐ 1-4
☐ 5-10	☐ 5-10	☐ 5-10
☐ 11+	☐ 11+	☐ 11+

I find the pricing of VIZ products to be: **(please check one)**

☐ Cheap ☐ Reasonable ☐ Expensive

What genre of manga and anime would you like to see from VIZ? **(please check two)**

☐ Adventure ☐ Comic Strip ☐ Science Fiction ☐ Fighting

☐ Horror ☐ Romance ☐ Fantasy ☐ Sports

What do you think of VIZ's new look?

☐ Love It ☐ It's OK ☐ Hate It ☐ Didn't Notice ☐ No Opinion

Which do you prefer? **(please check one)**

☐ Reading right-to-left

☐ Reading left-to-right

Which do you prefer? **(please check one)**

☐ Sound effects in English

☐ Sound effects in Japanese with English captions

☐ Sound effects in Japanese only with a glossary at the back

THANK YOU! Please send the completed form to:

NJW Research
42 Catharine St.
Poughkeepsie, NY 12601

All information provided will be used for internal purposes only. We promise not to sell or otherwise divulge your information.